How to Make a Visit

Eliminating Fears and Breaking Down Barriers With Time-Tested Tips That Work

Kurt Johnson

Pacific Press®
Publishing Association
Nampa, Idaho | www.pacificpress.com

Cover design Michelle C. Petz
Inside design by Trent Truman / TrumanStudio.com

The author assumes full responsibility for the accuracy of all facts
and quotations as cited in this book.

You can obtain additional copies of this book by calling toll-free
1-800-765-6955 or by visiting http://www.adventistbookcenter
.com.

Library of Congress Cataloging-in-Publication Data

Names: Johnson, Kurt W., 1950- author.
Title: How to make a visit / Kurt W. Johnson.
Description: Nampa, Idaho : Pacific Press Publishing Association, 2020. |
    Summary: "A short guide for making visits to Bible study contacts,
    former members, and sick members"— Provided by publisher.
Identifiers: LCCN 2020031372 | ISBN 9780816366880 |
    ISBN 9780816366897 (kindle edition)
Subjects: LCSH: Visitations (Church work)
Classification: LCC BV4320 .J64 2020 | DDC 253/.76—dc23
LC record available at https://lccn.loc.gov/2020031372

August 2020

CONTENTS

PREFACE

And with great power the apostles gave witness to the resurrection of the Lord Jesus. And great grace was upon them all.—Acts 4:33

During my lifetime I have had the privilege of visiting the homes of people in need of the forgiving grace of Christ. My own visitation ministry experience has been developed and honed by the Holy Spirit and by those with whom I have had the privilege of serving in ministry as I have gone from home to home. This book reflects God's guidance, my own personal experiences, and principles I've learned over the years from my colleagues in ministry.

It is my desire that as you read the pages of this book, you will glean a few "visitation pointers." Experience has taught me that you might have a different thought or idea from what I share in these pages, and that is OK. There is more than one way to accomplish visitations. That is why God has created each of us different. Together, combining our efforts and approaches, we can prepare more people for His kingdom!

I am praying for you as you reach your community for Jesus. May you serve Jesus with "great power" and experience the "great grace" (Acts 4:33) that only comes through walking with Him.

1

READY OR NOT

I had finished my final class in college, the last textbook had been closed, and the moving van driver had unloaded my few boxes of belongings at an apartment in Portland, Oregon. A few days later, I was standing with Carl on the front porch of a house.

"Kurt, Hazel is hard of hearing, but she should answer that knock on her door."

Leaning close to the door, Carl shouted, "Mrs. Smith, are you home? It is Carl with your Bible lesson."

No answer.

About that time, the next-door neighbor, who was sweeping off her porch, peered over at us and asked, "May, I help you?"

Carl's face was one big smile as he responded, "Yes, I was looking for Mrs. Smith. I stop by each week at this time and bring her a Bible lesson. She is usually home."

The neighbor responded cautiously, "She had an early doctor's appointment, but I am sure she will be home soon."

I smiled my goodbye, turned, and was walking to the car when I heard Carl say, "My name is Carl. Hazel really enjoys these Bible lessons. Would you like to understand the Bible better? I would be happy to give you a Bible study guide."

Pausing mid stride, I turned and saw Carl walking toward his newfound friend. I sheepishly wandered back and stood there watching Carl explain how to study the Bible and find the Bible texts by page number with the Bible that accompanied the study guide.

After we got back in the car, Carl beamingly said, "Oh my, isn't God good! Mrs. Smith wasn't home, but we got to meet her neighbor. You have to be ready because God always has someone He has been preparing to study the Bible."

I learned a lot from Carl over the next few months. Most of what I learned, I learned by watching. I discovered why Carl was considered "one of the best" full-time Bible workers in North America. He had three keys to success. He never told them to me—I just figured them out by riding along. Here they are:

1. *Carl prayed earnestly before each visit.* I have to emphasize the word *earnestly*. I know because I listened to him pray and watched his dependence upon God. It was God who made the visit, and Carl was just His partner.

2. *Carl radiated friendliness.* He had a smile the size of a banana! Even when someone declined a Bible study or their reception to the visit was not the best, the person being visited knew Carl genuinely cared.

3. *Carl always believed—and knew by experience—that God was ready to let him be part of what He was already doing in someone's life.* Carl never gave up! He was enthusiastic about ministry.

Carl's Bible knowledge was used by God to assist people to become fully devoted disciples of Jesus, but that was only part of the success.

You see, Carl's core value was that God was letting him be a part of what God was already doing in the lives of others. It was Carl's job simply to be friendly and find those ready to experience God.

I watched Carl apply this core value when we visited Fred, who had stopped attending church, then again when we visited Sarah in the hospital after her surgery, and, finally, as we visited Mary, who was homebound.

It made no difference the type of visit—the bottom line was that we were doing what Jesus said we were supposed to do. We are His hands, feet, and voice on this earth. We read this principle in John 17:18, "As You sent Me into the world, I also have sent them [you and me] into the world."

If you are like me when I first began visiting, you most likely are thinking, *That is all well and good, and I believe it. I would love to go visit someone, but I am still afraid. Fear has me handcuffed. What do I do?*

Keep reading.

2

SHARING YOUR FAITH WITHOUT FEAR
(OR AT LEAST PARALYZING FEAR)

Have you ever talked while your body was shivering from the cold air? Your coat and jeans shake, your teeth chatter, and your voice vibrates and quakes. You are cold to the bone and want to go inside and warm up. That is how I felt standing on the front steps of "Occupant Unknown" in Yuma, Arizona. I was not feeling cold air—after all, I was in Arizona! It was warm outside, but that did not keep me from being scared. The pastor had talked me into leaving pamphlets at people's doors while he drove the supply vehicle, making sure the other volunteers and I were well supplied with pamphlets.

Let's be honest—the last thing I wanted to do was talk to a stranger. But the pastor had asked, "If we don't do this, who will?" Guilt got the best of me, so there I was, doing the unthinkable. Most people don't believe me when I tell them I have a shy side. All they ever see is this smiling, talking, let's-go-make-this-happen kind of guy. It is true that I love people and that I enjoy hanging out with my friends. And I can start up a conversation and keep it going with someone I am meeting for the first time. But talking to a stranger about Jesus and the Bible did not come naturally. For a lot of us, fear can have a paralyzing effect.

But we read in Acts 5:32 that "we are His witnesses to these things."

And Mark 16:15 records, "And He said to them, 'Go into all the world and preach the gospel to every creature.'"

Let me ask you a question: Would God ask us to do something and then not help us accomplish it? Would He set us adrift and leave us all alone? I know your answer, because it is probably like mine, "No, He wouldn't, but . . ."

Let's look at the topic from this angle. As my pastor in Yuma asked the members of his congregation, "If you do not go, who will?" Now, we know that all have been given different witnessing gifts by God—that is plain enough in Scripture. But if a neighbor or friend at work asks you a question about a biblical topic or asks why you are a Christian, you will need to answer. If someone in your community requests a Bible study or other type of assistance, someone needs to make the visit.

I know from personal experience that fear destroys one's self-confidence. As Job expressed it, "The thing I greatly feared has come upon me" (Job 3:25). I know I am applying his words a bit out of context, but you get the point! Let me share with you how I learned to not let fear keep me from talking to others about God.

Lesson 1: Depend upon God's Word

When God states something, believe it. Years ago, I copied down on pocket-sized cards the promises of God telling me He would give me victory over fear and send the Holy Spirit's power into my life. I carried the cards in my shirt pocket. Whenever I was going to make a visit, I prayed through the Bible texts written on the cards. Between visits, I read the cards—eventually, I memorized the texts.

Fear comes from Satan—it is a result of sin on this earth. A sound, calm mind is what God gives us. Jesus has overcome Satan, and when we accept

His salvation, God gives us a quiet, peaceful mind. Whenever Satan put a negative, fearful thought in my mind, I replaced it with a positive thought from God's Word. Even today, you will see me reading my pocket cards as I visit; or before I speak to a group, you might see me thumbing through the cards, claiming God's presence as I am getting ready to preach.

Here are some texts from those cards, several sets of which I have worn out over the years:

- "For God has not given us a spirit of fear, but of power and of love and of a sound mind" (2 Timothy 1:7).
- "There is no fear in love; but perfect love casts out fear, because fear involves torment. But he who fears has not been made perfect in love" (1 John 4:18).
- "Do not be afraid, but speak, and do not keep silent; for I am with you, and no one will attack you to hurt you" (Acts 18:9, 10).
- "Peace I leave with you, My peace I give to you; not as the world gives do I give to you. Let not your heart be troubled, neither let it be afraid" (John 14:27).

Lesson 2: Remember that God has asked us to share with others what we have personally experienced

A witness is someone with something to tell, someone who simply shares what they have seen, heard, or read. It is true, if a witness can spend some time outlining and preparing their story so it is presented as effectively as possible, the impact is usually greater. As we gain experience sharing with others, experience helps us relax, remember Scriptures, and express ourselves more clearly. Jesus promised, "Most assuredly, I say to you, he who believes in Me, the works that I do he will do also; and greater works than these he will do, because I go to My Father" (John 14:12).

Lesson 3: Do not attempt to do God's part

The program was over for the evening. My speaking appointment was completed and I was sitting in a chair with my legs outstretched, listening to Sherri, one of the evening's singers, tell me of her experience. Sherri belonged to a different church denomination than mine.

As I listened, my heart was aching and I became frustrated about what I was hearing. Sherri shared with me how angry she was with a couple of individuals who belonged to my church and who, in sharing their doctrinal beliefs with her, told her bluntly she was wrong in her beliefs. At every opportunity, they would shower her with Bible texts to prove to her she was wrong and they were right. Sherri blurted out, "Even if they are correct, I would never belong to their church. All they do is make me feel upset and angry!"

In their witnessing zeal, the two individuals had built an impenetrable wall rather than a bridge.

You don't need to pressure people, learn "sales pitches," or figure out the best arguments. It is the Holy Spirit that convicts hearts—period. Not you, not me. Let God do His part and relax in knowing that as you speak with others, God was there first.

When God convicts someone's heart, they will make a decision for Him—not before, no matter what you say or do. So, say to yourself, "I am going today as God's visiting partner. God will use me today as He chooses. It is not I who will impress someone else's heart, it is God. It is my responsibility to provide the person an opportunity to meet God by showing them that I care about them as a person and friend. As I visit, I will look for an opportunity to help meet the person's daily and eternal needs through a Scripture promise, some literature, or a Bible study. If they are not ready for these items, I will be their friend and pray for God to prepare their heart to respond to Him."

God has everything under control. Listen to these promises:

- "However, when He, the Spirit of truth, has come, He will guide you into all truth" (John 16:13).
- "It shall come to pass that before they call, I will answer; and while they are still speaking, I will hear" (Isaiah 65:24).
- "Christians are set as light bearers on the way to heaven. They are to reflect to the world the light shining upon them from Christ."[1]
- "The Saviour knew that no argument, however logical, would melt hard hearts or break through the crust of worldliness and selfishness."[2]

Lesson 4: Preparation is essential

One of the reasons we are fearful is because we are not sure what to say to the person with whom we are visiting. Preparing as much as possible regarding what you will say in your opening statement and determining what you want to accomplish during a visit will help you relax. It may not alleviate your fear completely, but it will help reduce it. As you gain experience, your nervousness will dramatically reduce. We will cover the topic of preparation in a later chapter.

Lesson 5: Be excited to fulfill the call of God

Because God has asked us to share with others about Bible truth, which includes His love for them, there is a peace that comes from knowing we are doing His will. It is true that some people we talk to will not be interested and some will not be as friendly as we would like, but we should be willing to participate no matter the response.

As you visit, have a passion for what you are sharing. Be excited about it. Show this excitement in your voice, your smile, and your kindness. This will reduce your fears and bring out the friendliness of the person you are visiting.

Lesson 6: Have a positive outlook about the person you are visiting

Once, when I was coordinating visitation teams during a prophecy seminar, a man named Jim kept writing on his response card, "This is Jim, and I want to be baptized."

I asked Sam, the person assigned to visit Jim, how the visit went.

Sam responded, "I don't think he really is interested in accepting Jesus and being baptized. He is just writing that on the card."

I asked, "Did you ask Jim if he had accepted Jesus into his life? Did you lead him in a prayer of acceptance?"

Sam replied, "No."

I then said, "Sam, please go back to Jim and lead him in a prayer of acceptance of Jesus. Believe that what Sam is saying is what he means. He might not be expressing himself in the same words you would use." Sam went back and after talking further with Jim, he recognized Jim's sincerity and they set up a date for his baptism.

Consider the following questions and their biblical answers:

- Does God want everyone to have a better life now through a relationship with Him?

"I have come that they may have life, and that they may have it more abundantly" (John 10:10).

- Does God want everyone to be saved eternally?

"[God] desires all men to be saved and to come to the knowledge of the truth" (1 Timothy 2:4).

"The Lord is not slack concerning His promise, as some count slackness, but is longsuffering toward us, not willing that any should perish but that all should come to repentance" (2 Peter 3:9).

"And you shall call His name Jesus, for He will save His people from their sins" (Matthew 1:21).

- Does God answer prayer according to His will?

"And whatever you ask in My name, that I will do, that the Father may be glorified in the Son" (John 14:13).

"Now this is the confidence that we have in Him, that if we ask anything according to His will, He hears us" (1 John 5:14).

- Does God want you to share Him with others?

"As You sent Me into the world, I also have sent them [you and me] into the world" (John 17:18).

- Does God want you to encourage others?

"Therefore comfort each other and edify one another, just as you also are doing" (1 Thessalonians 5:11).

- Does God want us to visit and encourage those in need?

"Pure and undefiled religion before God and the Father is this: to visit orphans and widows in their trouble, and to keep oneself unspotted from the world" (James 1:27).

"For I was hungry and you gave Me food; I was thirsty and

you gave Me drink; I was a stranger and you took Me in; I was naked and you clothed Me; I was sick and you visited Me; I was in prison and you came to Me" (Matthew 25:35, 36).

- Does God answer our prayers when they are according to His will? "Therefore I say to you, whatever things you ask when you pray, believe that you receive them, and you will have them" (Mark 11:24).

Based upon God's promises and will for every person living on planet Earth, go positively to their home, hospital room, or wherever they might be, knowing they belong to Him. God's presence and scriptural promises go before you and with you, and they stay in the home after you leave, not because of you—but because of Him!

Lesson 7: Have a positive attitude about yourself and believe God is working in your life

Many go through life feeling inferior and inadequate. They look at their own abilities and limit themselves to only a fraction of what God wants to do through them. We might feel that our education or speech is inadequate or that someone else could do a better job, and we don't want to embarrass ourselves or the other person.

Moses felt this way, but God used him: "Then Moses said to the LORD, 'O my Lord, I am not eloquent, neither before nor since You have spoken to Your servant; but I am slow of speech and slow of tongue'" (Exodus 4:10).

In my personal experience, I have found that most people, sometime in their lives, feel some inadequacies. The key is what we do with these thoughts and feelings.

When I begin to fear or have doubts, I remind myself to depend upon what God says and not what I think. God says the following about you:

- *You are His child*: "But as many as received Him, to them He gave the right to become children of God, to those who believe in His name" (John 1:12).
- *You are His treasure*: "But you are a chosen generation, a royal priesthood, a holy nation, His own special people, that you may proclaim the praises of Him who called you out of darkness into His marvelous light" (1 Peter 2:9).
- *He is with you when you go through the fiery trials of life*:

    "Fear not, for I have redeemed you;
    I have called you by your name;
    You are Mine.
    When you pass through the waters, I will be with you....
    When you walk through the fire, you shall not be burned.
    Nor shall the flame scorch you. For I am the LORD your
    God" (Isaiah 43:1–3).

- *He would have died for you even if you were the only one on the earth*: "The relations between God and each soul are as distinct and full as though there were not another soul upon the earth to share His watchcare, not another soul for whom He gave His beloved Son."[3]

Why do we hesitate in *claiming* God's Word in our lives and witness? The Bible does not teach this type of Christian living. Ellen White notes,

"Some seem to feel that they must be on probation, and must prove to the Lord that they are reformed, before they can claim His blessing. But they may claim the blessing of God even now."[4]

When we put ourselves on probation, we look at ourselves as second-class citizens, inferior Christians and witnesses. Don't let your past mistakes cause you to be afraid of God. This is exactly what Satan wants you to do. Listen to what God has already done with your sins:

- "He will again have compassion on us,
  And will subdue our iniquities.
  You [God] will cast all our sins
  Into the depths of the sea" (Micah 7:19).

- "As far as the east is from the west, so far has He removed our transgressions from us" (Psalm 103:12).
- "Therefore, if anyone is in Christ, he is a new creation; old things have passed away; behold, all things have become new" (2 Corinthians 5:17).

Experience has shown me that

- if you believe that your sins are not forgiven,
- if you believe that you cannot be used of God,
- if you believe there is no one in your community searching for God,
- if you believe the person you are going to visit really is not interested in your visit or God, and

- if you believe you and your local church have nothing to offer the people of your community,

then you will *not* find success in bringing people to Jesus to meet their daily and eternal needs.

But

- if you believe that you are a child of God,
- if you believe you are a new creation in Jesus Christ,
- if you believe that Jesus lives within you by the power of the Holy Spirit,
- if you believe that the person you are going to visit is a child of God who needs Him,
- if you believe that in your community there are people searching for God,
- if you believe that you are to *go* in the name of Jesus Christ, and
- if you believe that God has prepared and is preparing people for your visit or conversation,

then your church will reap many people for an eternal relationship with Jesus Christ.

Lesson 8: Christ works in us and through us

In the story of Balaam, God spoke through a donkey (Numbers 22:28). He also told us that He could make the rocks cry out (Luke 19:40). He also created the salmon that leaves its place of birth in an inland river, swims hundreds of miles into the ocean, and then returns to its place of birth as an adult salmon. And He made the arctic tern, which flies thousands of miles on its yearly migratory route and returns to its place of origin. *Our God who does all these things can speak through you or me.*

We read in the Bible, "For it is not you who speak, but the Spirit of your Father who speaks in you" (Matthew 10:20). In *Steps to Christ*, we read, "More than this, Christ changes the heart. He abides in your heart by faith. You are to maintain this connection with Christ by faith and the continual surrender of your will to Him; and so long as you do this, He will work in you to will and to do according to His good pleasure."[5]

A text that has encouraged my heart is Galatians 2:20, which states, "I have been crucified with Christ; it is no longer I who live, but Christ lives in me; and the life which I now live in the flesh I live by faith in the Son of God, who loved me and gave Himself for me." This is a key point to grasp and understand. Jesus lives within you through the Holy Spirit. Jesus also has perfect faith. Thus, when Jesus lives within you with His perfect faith, and you accept and depend upon His perfect faith united with your limited faith, He takes over—and that is why with God all things are possible!

Grasp this point, live this point, and self-dependence will be gone. Fear will be gone. You will be able to "do all things through Christ" (Philippians 4:13).

Remember to claim God's promises through prayer. When you do, God, who is faithful, will use your witness for Him.

---

1. Ellen G. White, *Steps to Christ* (Washington, DC: Review and Herald®, 1977), 115.
2. Ellen G. White, *The Acts of the Apostles* (Nampa, ID: Pacific Press®, 2005), 31.
3. White, *Steps to Christ*, 100.
4. White, 52.
5. White, 62, 63.

3

MAKING THE VISIT

I knocked timidly on the door of a house three blocks from my home. I was a senior in high school and was wishing I were pulling weeds, mowing grass, cleaning toilets, washing dishes, or doing all kinds of chores that I tried to get out of doing as a kid. I would do almost anything to *not* be standing on that front porch. As the door opened, a sweet-smiling grandma greeted me. I drew a sigh of relief and stumbled through a best-I-could-do offer of free Bible study guides.

As I walked off her porch, I breathed a sigh of relief. Only four more houses to go and I would be done. Hopefully, I would not meet any macho men or kids my own age—I preferred kind, cookie-sharing, hot-chocolate-giving grandmas.

One key reason we fear visiting someone is the unknown. We are not sure what the situation will be like. Too often, we picture the worst in our minds. We wonder if we will say the "right" words or "embarrass" ourselves or the person we are visiting.

No matter the type of visit—whether it is someone with an illness or hospitalization, a nonattending church member, a Bible-study request, or a general visit—there is one foundational principle that makes visiting much easier. In the book *Gospel Workers*, we read this principle: "Your success will not depend so much upon your knowledge and accomplishments, as upon your ability to find your way to the heart. By being social and coming close to the people, you may turn the current of their thoughts more readily than by the most able discourse."

The principle in this statement is this: Be a friend. Smile. Show people that you care about them! This quotation has always encouraged me. Notice the key points:

- Your ability to "find your way to the heart" of a person is more important than your "knowledge and accomplishments."
- Being a true friend to someone by "being social" and "coming close" is more powerful in changing someone's life for Jesus than the best-preached sermon.

Honest, heartfelt friendship is the core value of making a visit! It is not Bible knowledge, it is not being able to make the best speech, it is not your education that makes your visit life changing for someone; it is simply being a friend. Be a genuine heart-to-heart friend to someone. It is true that once your friendship is established, your understanding of the Bible and your love for God will make a difference in the lives of those you visit, but friendship is key.

Four steps to follow in preparing to make a visit

There are four steps in preparing for your visit. These steps apply to every type of visit:

- *Step 1*: Determine your goal or purpose for the visit.
- *Step 2*: Gather information about the person you are going to visit.
- *Step 3*: Pray for the person, the visit, and yourself.
- *Step 4*: Make the visit as a team of two, if possible.

Let's now review each step in detail.

Step 1: Determine your goal or purpose for the visit

Under this first step there are two categories. These are general goals that apply to every visit and specific goals for the type of visit you are making. First, let's look at the general goals.

General Goals

The following principles are good general goals to have in mind as you interact with others, no matter the type of visit you are making:

- *Establish a friendship with the person.* The number one goal of a visit is not to deliver a Bible guide or get a person to return to church but to show them you care about them as a person. When someone knows you truly care about them, then they will open their innermost thoughts to you. Friendship breaks down barriers. Argument builds walls.
- *Meet the personal needs of the person being visited.* The person you visit may be lonely, hungry, grieving, discouraged, or upset. If this is the case, then your first priority is to meet their needs if possible. Maybe you will need to assist with obtaining food for a family or transportation to a doctor's appointment or provide a listening ear. A person's immediate need is usually the priority in their life. Once the need is met, they will be ready to listen to you or begin their Bible study. We often forget that people in social, physical, mental, or economic difficulties may be too distressed to listen or make sound decisions about what we are presenting.

We must be prepared to help people in whatever condition we find them.

- *Look for opportunities to share what Jesus has done for you in your life.* I am not talking about a full descriptive story of your journey to becoming a Christian. If that opportunity arises, then share a brief version. Rather, I am recommending looking for opportunities—a window in the conversation to point the individual to God. For example, someone might say, "My life is so stressful and busy, I do not know what to do about it." You might respond, "I know what you mean. I am thankful God has told us we can bring our problems to Him in prayer and He will help us with our needs. It sure has helped me!"

- *Look for opportunities to lead someone to accept Jesus as Lord and Savior of their life.* This usually will not take place in the first visit. However, always be attuned to someone wanting to accept Jesus for the first time or desiring to recommit their life to Him. As Christians, we should be prepared to share what God has done for us in our lives and how someone can have the same experience.

Specific Goals

For every visit you are about to make, always ask yourself the following three questions. These questions and your answers to them will prepare you for how to approach the person:

1. Why am I going? (Determine the purpose of your visit.)
2. What do I want to accomplish? (Identify the goals of your visit.)

3. What am I going to say? (Think about your opening sentence.)

In addition, every person you visit—unless they know you or an appointment has been made with them—will have three questions in their mind when you knock on their door. Those questions are:

1. Who are you?
2. What do you want?
3. How long are you going to stay?

You can answer these questions in the first two sentences, as you will see in the illustrations that follow:

1. Visiting someone who requested Bible studies

    Why are you going?

    > To deliver the Bible lessons

    What do you want to accomplish?

    > To explain to the person how the Bible study process works, start the Bible study, and make an appointment to return

    What are you going to say?

    > "Hi, I am Kurt Johnson, and this is Denny James. Are you Bill Steinwig? You requested the free Bible guides, and we have brought them to you. Do you have a few minutes for us to explain to you about the Bible study guides? We won't stay long."

2. Visiting someone who is in the hospital following surgery

Why are you going?

To pray with them, to bring encouragement, and let them know you care

What do you want to accomplish?

To let them share, if they choose, about how they are doing and their current situation, read a Bible text that is a promise of hope, pray with them, and find out if there is anything you can do to assist them and their family

What are you going to say?

"Hi, Mary. Donna and I wanted to stop by and see how you are doing. I know you have been through a lot this past month—and especially the past few days with your surgery. We can't stay long, but we wanted to stop by and check on you. How are you today?"

Let the person share as much or as little as they choose. Be a good listener.

Once they are finished sharing, ask, "Mary, is there anything we can do to help you?" If you know the situation, ask about specific items, such as mowing the grass at her home, watering her flowers, and so on.

"Mary, we don't want to tire you, so I will read a verse from the Bible, pray, and then we will go."

3. Visiting someone who has not attended church for several weeks

Why are you going?

To let them know they are missed

What do you want to accomplish?

To let them know you care about them. If there is a need to meet or a problem to solve, you want to be available to assist if they ask.

What are you going to say?

"Hi, Kevin, it is good to see you. I just stopped by to see how you are doing. I have missed you at church the past month, and I wanted to make sure you were OK."

The key in this type of visit is not to probe or put the person in the "hot seat" about where have they been, as you have not seen them in church. You simply want to let them know you have missed them. If the person shares a simple answer and changes the subject, then follow their lead. If they go deeper into the reason for their absence, then follow along and be available to assist them with whatever the issue might be.

When I am leaving their home, depending upon the reason they have shared with me about why they have not been attending church, I simply say, "I will see you at church next week," or, "I will see you in a couple of weeks." The response you make as you leave will be dependent upon what the individual has shared with you.

If there are further follow-up visits needed or the person needs assistance, then it is important to act quickly on the information you have received. If you wait too long, the situation or difficulties could worsen.

Step 2: Gather information about the person you are going to visit
In this step, you are seeking information about someone to determine what has been their interest in the past on spiritual topics. Their past

involvement in Bible studies, attending community events such as health seminars, and visiting your local church will determine your approach in the visit. Check your church interest and membership file. Talk to church members who have lived in the community for many years. Also, do not forget to check social media. Many people post details of their daily lives and the information may be helpful as you make your visit.

Step 3: Pray for the person, the visit, and yourself

The topic of prayer as the foundation to visitation is so important that it has its own chapter (see chapter 7). However, to summarize here, pray for the guidance of the Holy Spirit, the home environment, your fears, your words, and the person you are going to visit. Ask God to be in charge of the visit.

Step 4: Make the visit as a team of two if possible

Jesus sent out the disciples in teams of two. Having a visitation partner provides encouragement and support. While one is talking, the other is praying. While one is talking, the other is thinking of Bible verses or comments to add to the discussion. Before the visit, always decide which partner is going to lead out in the visit. Both people cannot lead; otherwise, the visit will be chaotic. Discuss the visit with your partner before you arrive. Agree together on what the goals will be for the visit and what you want to accomplish. The lead person for the visit does just that—they lead. The partner is involved in the visit, but they take a secondary role.

For example, if there are children in the home and they are seeking Mom's attention during the Bible study so that it is difficult to conduct the study, the partner can entertain the children. If there is a nonparticipating spouse, the partner can talk with them to establish a friendship. The role of the partner is to be an assistant wherever the need arises.

With these principles in mind, let's now discover how to make the specific types of visits.

---

1. Ellen G. White, *Gospel Workers* (Hagerstown, MD: Review and Herald®, 2005), 193.

4

VISITING SOMEONE WHO HAS REQUESTED BIBLE STUDIES

Mary and Carolyn stopped by for a first-time visit to Rosalyn, who had requested Bible studies. When they knocked on Rosalyn's door, they were met with a stern look and a rough voice telling them, "I don't want your Bible studies."

As Mary and Carolyn made their way to their car, Rosalyn called to them, "Please come back, I have something for you."

Mary turned and began walking back to the door. Carolyn, who was making her "first-time *ever*" visits that day, thought Mary was crazy! Was it safe to go back to the door? Who was this lady, anyway?

Rosalyn said to them, "I have a small item that I make for sharing my faith and I want to give one to each of you. That is the least I can do after talking so strongly to you."

Standing inside the door, Carolyn was not sure what was going to happen—she wanted to be somewhere else. But Mary started up a conversation with Rosalyn. Rosalyn shared that the reason she was so harsh to them was because a gentleman had already stopped by that day offering Bible studies and she told him, "No, thank you." She thought that Mary and Carolyn were the second wave of attack!

After the getting acquainted and receiving the gifts from Rosalyn, Mary showed Rosalyn the Bible guides. Rosalyn agreed to a weekly Bible study appointment. Not long after the Bible studies started, Rosalyn invited four friends to join the Bible study. The group of ladies attended a Revelation seminar. There was heartfelt joy when Rosalyn along with Carolyn were baptized on a Friday evening at the conclusion of the meetings.

You see, Carolyn was attending church but had not fully committed her life to Jesus. Mary talked her into coming along with her that Sunday afternoon. Through Carolyn being part of a Bible study team, God spoke to Carolyn's heart, and she decided to follow Him. Today, giving Bible studies to those who request them is a regular part of Carolyn's life. Carolyn says that if *she* can visit someone and lead out in a Bible study, she knows anyone can!

I am going to share with you the steps I take in preparing to make a visit to someone who has requested Bible studies. I will illustrate in the following sections by using some of the principles I shared in chapter 3. These principles apply to every type of visit.

The setting

You have received an enrollment card in the mail from someone in your community requesting free Bible guides. The person's name is Linda. You are now preparing to make the visit.

Here are some basic principles to remember:

- *Depend on the Lord*. Prepare with prayer and pray before, during, and after the visit.

- *Your objective is to (1) be brief and get the person to receive and study the lessons, (2) make an appointment to return, and (3) begin a friendship.* Do not argue about anything. Your goal is to build bridges, not walls.
- *Know basically what you are going to say.* We will cover this point later in this chapter.
- *Dress appropriately.* The section of the country and the location the person lives in will determine how you dress. You want to dress like the people in the community you are visiting. You do not want to appear as an "outsider" or "odd." We are to be distinctive as Christians, but this does not mean being different in a negative way.

When I was visiting farmers in the wet Pacific Northwest, I, many times, had a muddy driveway to walk through or needed to head out to the barn or workshop. I always carried a pair of knee-high rubber boots in my car. I did not wear my suit but a pair of relaxed slacks or khakis that a little mud or horse hair did not bother.

Always dress modestly so the attention is on what you are saying and not on what you are wearing.

I had a friend who once went on a visit with his visitation partner, and both men had on dark suits. The person being visited thought they were law enforcement officers and headed out the back door!

- *Smile when the person opens the door.* This puts them at ease and lets them know you are a caring person. Our favorite news personalities are those who can share information in a friendly, relaxed manner with a smile on their face; that is, if the news is not a serious segment.

- *When you knock on the door, smile and be cheerful.* Do not stand close to the door. Knock and then take a couple of steps back so when the person opens the door, there is a comfortable space between them and you.

What to say at the door

As I mentioned in a previous chapter, there are three questions you need to answer before you make a visit. These are:

1. Why am I going?
2. What do I want to accomplish?
3. What am I going to say?

Also, as previously mentioned, when you knock on the person's door, there are three questions that arise in their mind (unless they know you are coming):

1. Who are you?
2. What do you want?
3. How long are you going to stay?

These three questions determine your opening remarks when you make the visit.

Let's now process these six questions. Remember, we are going to visit Linda, who has mailed in a Bible study enrollment card offering free

Bible study guides. Let's answer our questions.

1. Why are we going to Linda's home?

     To take Linda the free Bible study guides she requested

2. What do we want to accomplish at Linda's home?

     We want to give her the Bible guides, explain how to study the guides, and make an appointment to return.

3. What are we going to say when Linda opens the door to her home? (Remember, as we discussed earlier, that our answer to this question will depend on Linda's three internal questions when she hears our knock.)

     A. Who are you?

          "Hi! I am Kurt Johnson and this is Anna, we are with the _____ Bible School. Are you Linda?"

     B. What do you want?

          "Linda, you mailed in this card [show her the card] requesting free Bible study guides, and we have stopped by to bring them to you."

     C. How long are you going to stay?

          "Do you have a few minutes?"

My opening statement explains quickly to Linda who we are, what we want, and how much time we need. This helps Linda relax because all of us now know that we are at Linda's house because she requested the Bible studies. This helps make our visit nonthreatening to Linda.

Before we visit Linda, there are several things we should do: For our files, we need to use a copy machine or scanner to make a copy of the Bible-study enrollment card that Linda mailed in. The reason is that sometimes, when the visitor shows the card to the person who mailed it in, the person wants to keep the card. A copy ensures that the visitor has a record of the request.

We also need to take these three items with us to the door:

1. The enrollment card the person returned in the mail. We are going to show them the card at the door to remind them about sending it in, as sometimes people forget.
2. A copy of guide number 1 of the Bible guides the person requested.
3. A stamped return envelope with our local Bible school address on it. The reason is that the person might tell us they want to study by correspondence, so this way we will have an envelope for this purpose.

In our car, we also should have extra enrollment cards and several extra copies of guide number 1 from the set of Bible guides that we are using. When we make the visit, there might be other family members interested in the Bible guides. (I know some visitors do not carry extra items with them, as it offers another opportunity for a return visit if more Bible guides are needed.)

What to say at the door

"Hi! I am [your name] with the _____ Bible School. Are you [share the name on the enrollment card]? We received this card, which you sent in requesting the free Bible guides. [Show the person requesting the Bible lessons the enrollment card.]

"I can't stay long, but I have stopped by to bring you the first Bible guide and to answer any questions you may have. Do you have a few minutes?

"The Bible guide is easy to complete. Simply read through the study guide—the key Bible texts are written out to make it easy for you. However, you can look up the texts in your Bible, and there is a word search section with additional texts for you to find in your Bible. At the end there is an answer sheet, which you can fill out. That is all there is to it! It is very simple and interesting to read.

"What I'd like to do is leave the first Bible guide. I can come back in a week and review your answer sheet with you and discuss any questions you may have. I will also bring you the next Bible study guide. How does that sound to you?"

If the person responds positively, then set up the appointment for the next week. If the person is excited you are there, then ask them if they would like to have a personal, one-to-one Bible study together or be part of a small-group Bible study. If they answer in the affirmative, then at your second visit, you will complete the Bible-study guide together. (For further instruction, see the booklet *How to Give a Bible Study* by Kurt Johnson.)

Sometimes the student responds with statements or questions. Following are the most common questions and statements and a suggested response:

"I thought the lessons would come in the mail." If they say, "I thought the lessons would come in the mail," respond by saying, "I usually stop by to explain the process. However, I can send the lesson in the mail

or I can come by each week. Which do you prefer?"

If the person shows some resistance to having you come to their home, arrange to have them return the answer sheet to the Bible school by mail. Give the person a return envelope with your Bible school address on it. Then tell them that future guides will be sent to them in the mail.

"Which denomination sponsors these Bible study guides?" If they ask which denomination is sponsoring the lessons, say, "The lessons are from the [name of] ministry, sponsored by the Seventh-day Adventist Church. Some of the favorite topics of Bible students are included in these Bible guides and are designed for people of all faiths."

"I already belong to a church." If they say, "I am a [name of religion or denomination], so no thank you," respond by saying, "These lessons are designed for people of all faiths and are based only on the Bible. Why not try the first couple of lessons?"

"I did not fill out the card. This is not my handwriting." If the person says, "I did not fill in the card. That is not my handwriting; I do not want the Bible guides," I usually respond as follows, depending upon the circumstances: "I am already here and many people really enjoy the guides, so why don't I leave it with you and you can see how you like it? I will contact you in a week and if you like the Bible guide, I will give you the second guide. If you do not like the guide, just tell me and that is OK too. Does that sound all right to you?"

If the person says, "No I do not want it," I say to them, "OK, no problem, it was nice meeting you. Sorry for the inconvenience. Have a nice day."

Prayer

If it seems appropriate before you leave, ask the person if you can have a brief prayer with them to ask God to bless them as they study the Bible guides: "Dear Lord, thank You for [name of person], who has a desire to study the Bible. Help them as they open Your Word to understand more fully Your plan for the future and their own life. Please bless and guide them. In the name of Jesus. Amen."

Conversations with people you do not know

In several of the chapters in this book, we discuss what to talk about when having conversations with people you are meeting for the first time. Of course, you will share with them the reason for your visit, but you also have the goal of developing long-term friendships with them.

When I first started making visits and was concerned with how to start a conversation with someone I did not know, a pastor told me that there are two acronyms that illustrate the process one follows, over time, in establishing redemptive friendships. These two acronyms are FORT and SHIRT. The FORT acronym is commonly used with adults and the SHIRT acronym is used more frequently when talking with youth.

The acronym for FORT is the following:

F = Family

O = Occupation

R = Religion

T = Testimony

The acronym for SHIRT is the following:

S = School

H = Hobbies, home

I = Interests

R = Religion

T = Testimony

The acronyms are used as guidelines in starting a conversation and eventually developing the conversation into spiritual discussions. For example, when talking with an adult and using FORT, you can begin conversations by asking questions about their *family*, such as: "Is that a photo of your family? How long have you lived here? Do you have pets?"

The next natural step is to ask about their *occupation*. For example, "What is your employment?"

When it is comfortable to do so, I ask, "What is your *religious* background? Did you attend a church growing up? Are you currently attending a church?"

As you make multiple visits, begin to look for windows of opportunity to share a brief *testimony* about God's leading in your life. For example, let's imagine that the person states, "I am having trouble communicating with my daughter. What would you do in my circumstance?" A response might be, "When I am faced with a difficulty, I talk to God about it in prayer. He has promised to assist us with problems in life and has done this for me in my life. One of my favorite verses states, 'before they call, I will answer' (Isaiah 65:24). Have you ever prayed before?" Depending upon their response, pray for them and show them how easy it is to pray. Eventually, invite the person to study the Bible, attend a seminar or church service, or to participate in a similar activity.

Once, I was visiting a lady named Lorrie. She was sharing with me about a number of difficulties in her life. I asked Lorrie if she would like for me to pray with her and she said yes. I bowed my head and began to pray. However, Lorrie interrupted me and said, "Kurt, I have never prayed before. What are we supposed to do?" I explained to Lorrie about God, prayer, and talking to God as we would to each other. I explained to her why I began with "Our heavenly Father." I shared why I ended my prayer with "in the name of Jesus, amen." I explained why I bowed my head and closed my eyes. After discussing how to pray, I then prayed. When I finished, Lorrie said, "That is the most beautiful thing anyone has ever done for me!" I explained to her that she could now talk to God every day at any time and He would guide her life. The lesson I learned was never assume everyone knows how to pray. Even the disciples said to Jesus, "Teach us to pray" (Luke 11:1).

The SHIRT acronym is similar to FORT, with the difference being that you ask a youth, "What school do you attend?" Then you can move on to the *H* in the acronym: "What are your hobbies or interests?" Also, look for opportunities to share your testimony and ask about the young person's religious background, as described previously.

Additionally, as you talk with both adults and youth, you can use any of the parts of both acronyms. These are simply discussion starters and ideas. Use what you believe is best for the situation.

Sharing your personal story

Every Christian has a personal story of how they first met God. Your story can be used by God to assist someone else in making a decision to accept

Jesus into their life as Lord and Savior. For example, during a conversation with a person about the plan of salvation, you can say, "There was a time when Jesus was not a part of my life," or, "I was fortunate to have been raised in a Christian home, but there was a time when I had to decide to accept Jesus into my life."

In planning what to say as you share your story, a simple outline can assist you in your preparation.

The outline has three parts:

1. Your life before you accepted Christ
2. The circumstances that led you to accept Christ into your life
3. Your life now as a Christian (e.g., the benefits and positive changes)

My suggestion is to follow the outline and write out your story. Once it is written, make a brief outline and practice by sharing it with a friend. Some basic guidelines are to share the least information regarding what your life was like before you became a Christian. We do not want to glorify Satan or a sinful lifestyle. So do not share details, but speak in more general terms. Spend most of your time on sharing how God has made a difference in your life. Share the benefits of the Christian life.

Prepare a three- or four-minute version and a ten-minute version of your story. Do not talk a long time when sharing your story. You want the person to listen and respond to God themselves, not wish you would quit talking.

Additional pointers

The suggestions I share in this particular section are based upon my personal experience. If you or someone else has a different opinion, that is OK too. Everyone must serve, as we say, wearing their own armor. But, hopefully, what I share in the following paragraphs will help you get started in visiting and be good discussion starters for your church group or visitation training class.

Should a person take a Bible to the door with them on the first visit? It depends. If a free Bible is part of the Bible study package, then, yes, bring it with you. You can always keep a few extra Bibles in your car and retrieve them as needed. If you carry a Bible to the door on the first visit with a stranger, and the person is still Bible or Christian shy, it might make them nervous. Use your judgment and do what is most comfortable for you.

Be mindful of your deportment and conversation. As you and your visiting partner approach the door, do not talk and laugh loudly. This can be troubling to the person being visited and actually harm their response to you and your opportunity for future visits. If you are talking as you approach the door, do so quietly and with smiles on your faces. Remember that many people today have video cameras recording everything.

Never peek through windows or doors. I have seen those making visits approach the door while staring into the large living room window pane to see if anyone is in the home. It is more appropriate to simply walk to the door as if the large window did not exist. You do not want embarrassing moments for anyone.

Treat the backyard as another room in the house. If no one answers the front door and you decide to approach the back door, or if you hear people in the backyard, treat that space as a room in the house. For many people, the backyard is private space. If there is a fence, do not walk into the yard, but stand at the fence and call to the person—especially if the fence is a tall wooden fence and you cannot see into the yard.

Remember that you are on personal property. When you make a visit to someone's home, once you leave the public street area, you are on their personal private property. As visitors, we need to respect their property. This means walking on the sidewalk, staying out of flower beds, and not doing things that will anger the homeowner. In some locations, situations, and cultures, it might be OK to walk across lawns and not use the sidewalk, but make sure it is acceptable. It might save time as you go to as many homes as possible, but your actions might build a barrier to the point that a homeowner might not want you to return.

Be discrete when you take notes after a visit. Do not sit in your car in front of the home after your visit to write down notes or to plan the next stop. The person you are visiting might observe you and wonder what you are writing down or why it is taking you so long to leave their driveway. Drive out of sight of the home of the person you were visiting, and then stop your car and write your notes or get directions for the next visit.

Be aware of no-soliciting signs. If you are not visiting a specific person and are walking door-to-door, then you will most likely encounter no-soliciting signs on some houses. If you are visiting a specific person who has requested Bible lessons or other materials, then ignore the sign. However, if you are walking door-to-door, then you need to be aware of the local regulations.

Most cities have specific regulations regarding the meaning of the phrase *no soliciting*. This meaning can vary by community. Some regulations prohibit the leaving of religious material and the making of religious visits and others do not. Some localities have monetary fines for violating the regulations. Call the city hall in each community regarding regulations.

Even if the regulation permits the leaving of religious materials when a no-soliciting sign is displayed, the person displaying the sign might think differently. The homeowner might point to the sign and be upset with you for visiting their home. If this occurs, be polite and do not argue. Simply say, "I am sorry. I contacted the city hall before I began visiting and they told me it was OK. I did not mean to disturb you." Or say, "I am sorry. I am not soliciting. I am giving material away. I have something free for you."

Another suggestion is to write down the addresses of the houses with no-soliciting signs and mail the material to them. Remember, your goal in making visits is to make friends and build bridges, not make enemies and build barriers.

Dealing with dogs and beware-of-dog signs. Once I made a visit to a man who had requested free Bible studies in response to an enrollment card mailing. I drove down a graveled country driveway and, arriving at the house, I proceeded to knock on the door. No one was home, so I left and returned a few hours later. The man was home on the second visit. This time, before I could open my car door, I was greeted by a barking, growling dog. The homeowner locked the dog in the dog pen and I got out of the car.

I told the man I had been there earlier and no one was home. He was amazed the dog had not bothered me on my first visit. He shared with me that the dog had recently cornered a visiting salesman on the hood of his car! The dog had let the man get out of the car and then charged him and the man jumped up on the hood of his car. A couple of hours later, the dog owner arrived home and freed the salesman.

My personal suggestion is if a dog is barking, growling, charging, or showing other threatening behavior, do not proceed into a fenced yard or get out of your car in a unfenced yard. If someone is home, they will usually come outside and take care of the dog. You can always come back if you have a reason for a specific visit. If you are walking door-to-door, then simply write down the address and mail the item with a note explaining about the item.

It is true that God, who shut the lions' mouths for Daniel, can shut the mouth of a dog, but I proceed with caution believing that God wants me to use good judgment too. On the flip side of my statement, I have also heard stories of God protecting someone from threatening dogs and the dogs' owner accepting Jesus into their life. That is why I always write down the address and contact the person by mail, including instructions on how to contact me for further information.

Never argue. Never, never, *never.* You may win an argument but lose a Bible study interest. Use statements such as, "Thank you for sharing your understanding," or, "I appreciate your viewpoint, but I understand it a little differently than you." In other words, respect the person's opinion. If you are too adamant against their opinion, a wall will be built instead of a bridge to introduce the person to Jesus as Lord and Savior of their life. Remember our earlier statement from *The Acts of the Apostles*? It is worth reading again, "The Saviour knew that no argument, however logical, would melt hard hearts or break through the crust of worldliness and selfishness."[1]

Here is another helpful statement: "One sentence of Scripture is of more value than ten thousand of man's ideas or arguments."[2]

How to treat fellow sinners

Sometimes we feel that we are not doing our Christian duty if we do not point out to people their "sins." In my personal experience, I have found that if I let the Holy Spirit bring up the subject, the person will deal with the issue. By that I mean let the Bible study guides and the Bible bring up the sinful issues in someone's life. If the person brings the topic up, then I talk about the issues with them. In some cases, I do bring up the issues of their addictions and habits, but this is once I have their confidence as a friend. If I bring up the issues to the person, I always keep in mind these pieces of counsel:

"It is always humiliating to have one's errors pointed out. None should make the experience more bitter by needless censure. No one was ever reclaimed by reproach; but many have thus been repelled and have been led to steel their hearts against conviction. A tender spirit, a gentle, winning deportment, may save the erring and hide a multitude of sins."[3]

"Oh, let no word be spoken to cause deeper pain! To the soul weary of a life of sin, but knowing not where to find relief, present the compassionate Saviour. Take him by the hand, lift him up, speak to him words of courage and hope. Help him to grasp the hand of the Saviour."[4]

God visits with you

Go in the assurance of the power of God as you make the visits. I know you can do it, because God never fails us when we are doing His will.

1. Ellen G. White, *The Acts of the Apostles* (Nampa, ID: Pacific Press®, 2005), 31.
2. Ellen G. White, *Testimonies for the Church*, vol. 7 (Mountain View, CA: Pacific Press®, 1948), 71.
3. Ellen G. White, *The Ministry of Healing* (Mountain View, CA: Pacific Press®, 1942), 166.
4. White, 168.

5

VISITING FORMER AND DISCOURAGED CHURCH MEMBERS

Bill knocked on the door of Judy's home. She opened the door and he introduced himself as being a member and pastor of the local Adventist church. Bill shared that he understood she had attended the local church twenty years prior and he was stopping by to meet her. Judy invited Bill into her home and then immediately said to him, "I might as well tell you why I stopped attending."

Bill listened to Judy as she described receiving a strong reprimand from another church member for something she had said. It became a rather heated battle of words. And when a couple of the local church elders and the pastor became involved, Judy felt that she was not treated fairly. She had stayed away for two decades.

As Judy finished sharing, Bill responded, "I am so sorry you were hurt. I apologize on behalf of the church that the problem was not satisfactorily resolved for you and was so upsetting. I want to invite you to come back to church.

"I am sure the current members would like for you to return. When I asked a couple of longtime members if they knew you, they said yes and told me it would be good if you would return."

They talked a little bit more. Bill asked about Judy's family and work career and looked at the photographs of family and friends in the room in which they were sitting. He then said, "I need to be going. Let's pray together."

After Bill prayed, he said, "Let me know if there is anything I can do to assist you." Judy thanked Bill for coming, and a couple of weeks later, he saw her sitting in the back row of the church. The members welcomed her, and she became a regular attendee once again. The purpose of visiting those who previously worshiped at one's local church is to let them know you genuinely care for them, that God cares for them. You want them to be a part of your church family. As we visit them, we sincerely want them to be an ongoing friend no matter their response.

Bill's experience with Judy is typical of many individuals who are no longer attending church. Very few have stopped attending because of theological differences. The majority do not attend because of *relationship* issues. In my personal experience, I have found several factors influence why church members no longer attend.

Some of the reasons for no longer attending church include the following:

- The person experienced poor interpersonal relationships. Someone hurt them by their actions or words.
- The person never bonded with the core group of the church; they felt left out.
- The worship and church program did not meet the person's needs.
- The person or family moved, got busy, and never transferred their membership or made a practice of attending church.
- The individual had a personal, negative work experience in

church institutions or organizations.

- The person felt guilt for lifestyle habits, such as drinking alcohol, doing drugs, smoking, and so on.
- The person received church discipline for moral issues, lifestyle choices, and related items.
- Young children or babies were hard to care for at church and the parents felt they disrupted the service. So the young parents decided to stay home until the children were older. Over time, they simply drifted away from the church.

In reference to these points, my observation reveals that when a person only attends church and is not involved with some volunteer activity of the church—even something as simple as setting up tables for the fellowship meal—it may impact their involvement and attendance.

People will attend a church where they feel they are wanted, they belong, and they are supported, even if the worship services aren't enhanced by theater-style lighting and a top-of-the-line audiovisual system. Caring people, willing to resolve differences and conflicts in a kind manner and willing to tell one another, "I am sorry," will go a long way in helping members continue attending.

When you make a visit to someone who is no longer attending church, introduce yourself as being a member of the church, and explain that you stopped by to get acquainted. Be warm and friendly, but not overly friendly. In many cases, the fact you stopped by might put them on their guard, since they do not know what you might say. Your goal is to make the person feel relaxed.

If I notice the person is really uncomfortable, I simply say, "I want you to know that I did not stop by today to pressure you. I truly want to become acquainted with you and let you know we would like for you to return to church and be part of the church family. I respect your feelings and opinions, and I simply want to be a friend. If you choose not to return to church, you are still my friend."

My goal is to help them relax and be comfortable with me as a person—hopefully, a friendship will develop. I make multiple visits as needed.

Whether you are invited into the house or not, you can ask some basic questions to become acquainted. These include: "How long have you lived here in [name of town]? What kind of work do you do?"

Once the person answers a couple of questions, I volunteer information about myself. I share with them how long I have lived in the area, I share about my work, and so on. The conversation needs to be mutual, not one-sided with the visitor asking all the questions!

If the conversation is progressing in a positive direction, then you can continue asking questions to get acquainted, such as these:

- "Do you have children or grandchildren? How many do you have?"
- "Do you have other family living in the area?"

If you are in the person's home and see photos, ask, "Are these photos of your family?" The person will usually begin talking about the family members in each photo. Sometimes there are photos of family vacations, or shelves are lined with golf trophies and other special items. Ask about these items and share information about yourself. In other words, do the things you normally do and say to become acquainted with someone. As I was writing this, I was sitting on an airplane. The lady across the aisle and her seatmate were just becoming acquainted. Both shared about where they lived, their flight destination, what they planned on doing when they landed, their work, and other general topics.

As we are becoming acquainted with each other, the person, without my asking, will sometimes automatically bring up why they no longer attend church. Many times, they state, "You probably would like to know why I no longer attend church." I respond, "If you are comfortable sharing with me, I would like to know."

If they do not volunteer the information, I ask, "How long ago was it that you attended church? Have you ever thought about returning to church? What stands in the way of your return?"

Our role is to *listen*, not to argue, not to take sides. Many times, as the person talks, it is like releasing pressure that has built up inside of them. They can be angry, sad, tearful. Again, your role is to listen. The circumstances and God's guidance to you during your visit determines what you say in response. For example, I have said to people:

- "I am sorry you were hurt."
- "I am sorry you were treated as you described. If I were treated like that, I would be upset too."
- "God will forgive you for your past. He wants you to spend eternity with Him."
- "God loves you so much that Jesus came to this earth and lived and died on the cross for you."

Once the person indicates they want to return to church, follow up on any items that need to be addressed to assist them on their journey to return.

If I am not invited into the house and the person appears to not want to talk as we stand on their front porch, then I simply say, "It was good meeting you. I would like to become better acquainted with you sometime. Have a good day." I will wait a few months and make a return visit unless the person has indicated that I should not return.

There are some basic principles, which we will examine in the following paragraphs, to keep in mind as you visit.[1]

Come to the point of your visit quickly

The person knows the purpose of your visit, so get to the point. Tell them in your introduction statement, "I am here because you once attended church, so I have stopped by to get acquainted with you."

This first visit is like a doctor's visit I made years ago. I had my first bout of vertigo and had to be physically supported by someone as I walked into the doctor's office. I was so dizzy I could not stand up. Everything around me was spinning, my stomach was upset, and I was all out of sorts. When the doctor saw me, his response was, "I recognize you. We went to college together!" He then proceeded to ask me questions about where I lived and other topics. I was thinking, *Hurry up and give me an inoculation or pills or something to cure my vertigo—I want to talk, but we can talk later!* That is exactly what the person you are visiting is likely thinking: *I know why you are here, so let's get to the point.*

Let the bitterness come out

Listen kindly and interestedly. In some cases, the person is correct. They were treated unfairly or hurt by a church member, by a decision of the local church board, by the elders, or by the church organization itself as their employer. Hindsight sometimes causes us as humans to wish we had handled a situation differently.

I have worked in ministry within the church structure for more than forty years. Every church member and leader is a sinner who makes mistakes. And at times, some of them hurt others by their actions, personality issues that arise, and other situations. We need to admit our mistakes and speak the words "I am sorry" a bit more frequently than we do.

My first year in ministry, a retired pastor in my congregation said to me, "Kurt, if the Lord does not come early in your lifetime and if you work for the church, or participate as a member, there will come a time when someone will treat you unfairly or you experience a negative situation. It is not a matter of if, it is a matter of when. When that happens to you, remember you are a child of God. You work for God, not for people. Do not let it destroy your relationship with God, your church, or your eternal life." I have learned he was completely correct.

There comes a time for each of us to simply apologize on behalf of the church, others, or ourselves for mistakes of the past and help the person experience the grace and love of God in the present and future. Do not be so proud or defensive that you cannot say, "I am sorry."

Don't defend anyone, including the church

Remember, you were not there when the event occurred to cause the person to stop attending. So do not have an opinion about something you did not personally experience. Besides, being defensive will put up a barrier, and you will be seen as part of the group that caused the original pain for the person. Listen, be kind and understanding, and let the love of God remove the pain, bitterness, and hurt. There comes a time to put the negative experience behind us.

Don't betray the person's confidence in you

Keep to yourself what they share with you. There is no need to tell anyone. If you share publicly—or with others confidentially, the story leaks out, and the person finds out—your credibility will be gone, and they most likely will not renew their relationship with God and the church.

Don't stay long

Unless the person decides to give you a long version of why they are not attending church, make the visit short. Ten to twenty minutes is sufficient for the first visit. You can always return another time. Do not wear out your welcome.

Always close with prayer

I usually say, "I need to be leaving, let me pray before I go." Pray a short prayer asking God to meet the needs of the person.

Extend an invitation

If it seems appropriate, invite the person to church or to another meeting the church may be hosting. Make the invitation casual and conversational. Your goal is to let the person know you care and are genuinely interested in them, not to pressure them to immediately decide to visit the church or another meeting. No matter their decision, continue your contact and develop a genuine friendship.

Leave immediately following prayer

Lingering sometimes can have a reverse effect on your visit and prayer. The prayer usually has an impact upon the person, so leave with God speaking to their heart through your prayer.

Mary's story

Mary was involved in children's ministries and was excellent with children. One Sabbath, one of the members confronted Mary and told her that she should not be working with children because she was not a good example.

To say the least, Mary was devastated. Mary, her husband, and their children stopped attending church for a number of years.

Some years later, Mary's nonattending family decided they needed to go back to church. A friend from the previous church they attended encouraged them to come back. The very first Sabbath back, one of the longtime members scolded Mary for not attending church over the previous years. The family did not return. They now attend another church where they are once again leaders in children's ministries. Remember the quotations at the end of the previous chapter regarding the principles on how to treat others, shared from the book *The Ministry of Healing*? We need to prayerfully ask God to help us apply these words in our personal interactions with others: have "a tender spirit, a gentle, winning deportment" and "take him by the hand, lift him up, speak to him words of curage and hope." This should be our desire in speaking to others and in our interactions with them.

The words of Jesus, if applied by all Christians, would save much heartache: "Judge not, that you be not judged. For with what judgment you judge, you will be judged; and with the same measure you use, it will be measured back to you. And why do you look at the speck in your brother's eye, but do not consider the plank in your own eye?" (Matthew 7:1–3).

There are circumstances where one must speak to someone regarding an issue, but there is an appropriate way to approach the situation without causing them to walk away permanently from church and maybe from God. I am thankful that "the LORD does not see as man sees; for man looks at the outward appearance, but the LORD looks at the heart" (1 Samuel 16:7).

The member at Mary's church should have followed in the footsteps of the prodigal son's father. When his son returned home, the father said, "Bring out the best robe and put it on him, and put a ring on his hand and sandals on his feet. And bring the fatted calf here and kill it, and let us eat and be merry; for this my son was dead and is alive again; he was lost and is found" (Luke 15:22–24).

Let us each choose to be gracious, kind, and openhearted to one another, remembering that "love suffers long and is kind" (1 Corinthians 13:4).

---

1. For more information, see Fordyce W. Detamore's writings, such as *Seeking His Lost Sheep,* on visiting nonattending members. I have shared in this chapter some helpful principles I gleaned early in my ministry from reading his material on this topic.

6

VISITING THOSE WHO ARE SICK

In Matthew 25, we read Jesus' words that those who are "blessed of My Father" (verse 34) are those who visit the sick. "I was sick and you visited Me" (verse 36). When an individual is temporarily sick or has a long-term illness, an encouraging visit is usually appreciated by them. However, make sure your timing for the visit is correct.

Not everyone who is sick wants people to visit them right away. When I had surgery on my knee and when I had gallbladder surgery, I told my family not to tell anyone outside of my immediate family, as I wanted to be left alone for the time being. I preferred not to talk, and I simply wanted to rest. Not everyone is like me, but many people like alone time to rest when they are recovering from surgery. When they are feeling better, the visit is appreciated.

In the book *The Ministry of Healing*, we read about this balance: "It is misdirected kindness, a false idea of courtesy, that leads to much visiting of the sick."[1] Those who are very ill should not have visitors, except a visit by the pastor or a close friend when the family or sick person indicates it is OK to visit.

There are many ways to express kindness, concern, and love without a visit. Email a message to a family member to print and share with the person. Or mail the sick person a card and write a message. I have found that when I write out a prayer and include it with a card or note, it means a lot to the person.

Only visit when you know it is acceptable to do so. I even ask my closest friends if it is OK for me to visit: Are they ready for visitors? When I am told it is all right to visit, I keep the following eight principles in mind:

1. *Make the visit brief.* A normal visit should be about ten minutes, and a long visit should be fifteen to twenty minutes. If the person I am visiting becomes talkative, I will stay a little longer, but I carefully watch the time as I do not want them to become tired.

2. *Do not be loud and boisterous.* To come with quietness, cheerfulness, kindness, and a smile on your face is the best way to make a visit.

3. Have a normal conversation. Talk friend-to-friend.

4. Do not bring up stories of people you know who suffered from a similar difficulty and had a negative experience. You are there to encourage, not to discourage.

5. Pay attention to other family members in the room or in a waiting room. When you pray, include them in your prayer.

6. Your purpose is to let the sick person know they are loved and that you and others at church care about them and are praying for them.

7. When I visit someone who is sick, I greet them, let them know I am sorry for their illness, and tell them I wanted to stop by for a few minutes to pray with them. I ask them how they are feeling. Are there any personal needs I or others can help them with, such as mowing their lawn or feeding their pets? I share a Bible

text—many times I write the text on a small piece of paper, read it to them, and then pray. I leave the slip of paper with the Bible text for them to keep.

8. Many times, someone who is sick will prefer not to discuss their illness, especially if the conversation would deal with sensitive, personal health problems. To walk into someone's hospital room and say, "What kind of surgery did you have?" or, "What is your health problem?" can be very embarrassing to the person one is visiting. Simply start the conversation by saying, "Hi, Jim. I wanted to stop by and let you know we care and are praying for you. How is your recovery coming? Is there anything I can do for you, such as mowing your lawn or running errands? I did not plan to stay long, so let me share a Bible verse with you, pray, and let you continue to rest."

Visiting someone who has a terminal illness is awkward for some. I know when I first began my ministry as a pastor, I was not sure what to say or do.

I was three months into my pastoral internship after graduating from college. I had no experience in hospital visitation. My only orientation was a two-week class taught by the chaplain at the local Adventist medical center. We talked about "what to say" and "what not to say" to people dealing with terminal illness and chronic diseases.

Sarah, a sister of one of the church members, had been diagnosed with a brain tumor. My senior pastor was unable to make a visit and asked me to meet with the family and pray with them prior to surgery. I knew that I would read a scripture and pray, but what else should I say?

What else should I do? I was not sure, and it made me a bit nervous.

At 6:00 A.M., I crowded into the surgery preparation room with Sarah's family. It was a somber time, as the prognosis for the success of the surgery was not good. There was even a chance that the attempted removal of the tumor could cause permanent brain damage and death. I shared briefly about the fact that our God, who created Sarah, could also heal her. I read a text and prayed.

Sarah survived the surgery, but the physicians were unable to remove the entire tumor and eventually it took her life. The good news was that Sarah had hope in the coming of Jesus and the resurrection.

After the surgery, during subsequent visits to Sarah and while sitting with the family outside of the intensive care unit, I learned some valuable lessons.

I learned that what meant the most to the family and Sarah was my presence. Most of the time, in fact, the less that was said, the better. The simple reading of a Bible text and a prayer thanking God for His presence, healing, and comfort is what meant the most. Here is a sample prayer, using Sarah's story as an example:

"Our Heavenly Father, we thank You today for Your love for each of us and for meeting our needs. We have placed Sarah in Your care and asked You to bring healing to her. We now place our hand of faith in Your hand of mercy, trusting You to perform Your will on her behalf. We long for the day that Jesus will come and we will not have suffering and pain any longer. May that day be soon is our prayer in the name of Jesus. Amen."

Later, I met Lisa, who had a terminal illness. I learned from Lisa to wait for the person to bring up the subject of death and the struggle they are going through. I let Lisa talk when she was ready and she brought up the subject. I learned that, like Sarah, Lisa did not need a sermon or exposé on dying—she needed someone to listen. I would give her opportunities to talk if she chose to. I would ask her, "Lisa, how are you doing today? Are you discouraged? How are you handling your pain? Is there anything you want to talk about?" If Lisa wanted to talk about her health situation, I had opened the door for her to talk. If she did not, that was OK too.

When Lisa knew that she only had a few weeks to live, I brought up the subject. We talked about death and the family she was leaving behind. We also talked about the resurrection and heaven.

I learned through my experience with Sarah and Lisa that what mattered most was my presence, listening ear, and prayers. The visits were not long, but each of them knew I would come if they called me.

The most important ingredients when visiting a sick person are your smile, your prayer, and letting them know you care about them. The Bible says that "men always ought to pray and not lose heart" (Luke 18:1). And if there is ever a time when people feel their need of prayer, it is when their health fails or there are other challenges.

God wants us to encourage the sick, the hopeless, the afflicted to take hold of the strength that God offers. God is just as willing to restore the sick to health now as He was in biblical times. There are numerous scriptures of promise:

- "They will lay hands on the sick, and they will recover" (Mark 16:18).
- "Is anyone among you suffering? Let him pray. Is anyone cheerful? Let him sing psalms. Is anyone among you sick? Let him call for

the elders of the church, and let them pray over him, anointing him with oil in the name of the Lord. And the prayer of faith will save the sick, and the Lord will raise him up. And if he has committed sins, he will be forgiven. Confess your trespasses to one another, and pray for one another, that you may be healed. The effective, fervent prayer of a righteous man avails much" (James 5:13–16).

- "Most assuredly, I say to you, he who believes in Me, the works that I do he will do also; and greater works than these he will do, because I go to My Father. And whatever you ask in My name, that I will do, that the Father may be glorified in the Son. If you ask anything in My name, I will do it" (John 14:12–14).

So, go visit those suffering from illness, bringing encouragement, love, and empathy as you point them to a God who created them and a God who restores.

---

1. Ellen G. White, *The Ministry of Healing* ((Mountain View, CA: Pacific Press®, 1942), 222.

7

PRAYER: THE FOUNDATION OF YOUR VISITS

There are things that God answers in prayer that He would not do if we did not ask. How do I know? Read these words:

- "Ask, and it will be given to you; seek, and you will find; knock, and it will be opened to you" (Matthew 7:7).
- "It is a part of God's plan to grant us, in answer to the prayer of faith, that which He would not bestow did we not thus ask."[1]

Prayer changes things. This is a fact of prayer. Our asking and God's doing provides automatic results.

The first step in making a visit—or living daily life, for that matter—is to pray, then pray again, and when you are finished, pray some more. It is a basic principle of sharing one's faith with others that prayer is the gateway to every resource of God. These resources include, but are not limited to, ministry by angels, the Holy Spirit's power, miracles, divine interventions, and the very words to speak when needed.

This should not surprise us, because God has promised:

- "It shall come to pass that before they call, I will answer; and while they are still speaking, I will hear" (Isaiah 65:24).

- "Now the Lord spoke to Paul in the night by a vision, 'Do not be afraid, but speak, and do not keep silent; *for I am with you*, and no one will attack you to hurt you; for I have many people in this city' " (Acts 18:9, 10; emphasis added).
- "If you ask anything in My name, I will do it" (John 14:14).

God will honor these promises for you as you make visits. He will go before you and with you, and He will be present in the home once your visit is concluded. You see, God shapes the world by prayer. He changes lives through prayer. The more people pray, the better life becomes. One may live in a society or visit a home that is surrounded by the influence of sin, but a person who prays lives in an atmosphere that frustrates Satan. The praying Christian is protected by the strength and support of a victorious Savior.

Jesus did not tell Christians to organize always, to equip always, to attend committees always, or to preach always. But we have been told to pray always. The greatest gift a Christian has to offer the world, the church, their family, or the person they are visiting is their personal life of prayer.

So, when you are preparing to make a visit, spend most of your preparation time praying about your visit and less time worrying about the details of the visit.

Are you

- fearful to knock on a stranger's door? Pray.
- not sure what to say at someone's door? Pray.

- thinking the visit did not go well? Pray.
- feeling alone as you visit? Pray.
- not sure God is listening when you pray? Then listen to this assuring promise once again until it is affixed in your mind: "The relations between God and each soul are as distinct and full as though there were not another soul upon the earth to share His watchcare, not another soul for whom He gave His beloved Son."[2]

An important part in growing in prayer is learning to take God at His word—to trust our lives and cares to Him. Listen to His words: "He shall call upon Me, and I will answer him; I will be with him in trouble; I will deliver him and honor him" (Psalm 91:15).

Prayer connects us with an able God!

So, go in faith, remembering that God has already been to the house before you arrive. We know because we asked.

Here are six things I have learned about visits and prayer:

1. *Pray for the Holy Spirit.* Ask God to go with you as you make the visit. Ask God to prepare the home environment and the people in the home for your coming. It is not our gifts or abilities that will make a difference in people's hearts and lives—but God Himself. He alone convicts hearts. Zechariah 4:6 is key: " 'Not by might nor by power, but by My Spirit,' says the Lord of hosts."

2. *Pray for wisdom.* You and I are human. We do not know the best approach or the correct words to say to bring healing to a person's troubled mind and life. Only God knows. As the Bible reminds us, "If any of you lacks wisdom, let him ask of God, who

gives to all liberally and without reproach, and it will be given to him" (James 1:5).

3. *Pray for sensitivity and tact.* When we are visiting someone, none of us wants to hurts their feelings, make them wish we would leave, or cause them more pain. However, at times we must be bold and straightforward. There is a balance. The wrong words or approach could build a wall and not a bridge. We must pray that God leads in the conversation and our choice of words and go in faith believing He will. "Now when they bring you to the synagogues and magistrates and authorities, do not worry about how or what you should answer, or what you should say. For the Holy Spirit will teach you in that very hour what you ought to say" (Luke 12:11, 12).

4. *Pray for God to remove your fear.* Many times, we are fearful that we will "ruin" the visit for God. We are not sure if we can answer the questions asked or deal with possible—but unlikely—confrontation. Follow the example of Peter and John. When they were confronted by the priests and Sadducees, their response was, "For we cannot but speak the things which we have seen and heard" (Acts 4:20). They also prayed, "Now, Lord, look on their threats, and grant to Your servants that with all boldness they may speak Your word" (Acts 4:29).

5. *Pray for the response of the people you are visiting.* We all want the people we visit to be happy to see us. We want them to be positively receptive to the reason for our visit. We want the recipients of our visit to desire us to return for another visit. Satan wants the opposite. Scripture tells us that Satan wants

to discourage and destroy: "The thief does not come except to steal, and to kill, and to destroy. I have come that they may have life, and that they may have it more abundantly" (John 10:10). We need to pray, claiming God's victory over Satan. Remember that Jesus said, "These things I have spoken to you, that in Me you may have peace. In the world you will have tribulation; but be of good cheer, I have overcome the world." (John 16:33).

6. *Pray for the home environment.* There are many things to create distraction in the home, such as nonstop sitcoms, game shows, and soap operas on television; social media on cell phones; and so many other things that scream for attention. Add to this list children and pets, and we are facing a host of potential disruptions to our visit. Put the home setting in God's hands and go knowing God is already there when you arrive.

A question that is often asked when I am teaching a seminar is, "Should I pray in every home or setting when I am visiting?" My answer is yes. Pray even if the situation to you seems awkward. Sometimes, when we arrive at a home, there are guests visiting. Because of the presence of guests, it might not be the appropriate time to bring up certain questions or share comments that you would make if the guests were not present. These might be left for another visit. However, when you leave, always pray.

I usually say something like, "Before I go today, let me pray with you." I always include the guest in my prayer. "Our Heavenly Father, I ask that you will be with Bill today. Thank you for meeting his needs and guiding his life. I am thankful to be able to meet his friend Alex today. Please also meet the needs of Alex's life. Watch over each of us and our family members. We ask this in the name of Jesus, amen."

H. M. S. Richards Sr., the founder and speaker of the Voice of Prophecy ministry, said that he learned very early in his ministry to always pray, even in circumstances that might seem awkward to him. Pastor Richards and his best friend at Campion Academy in Loveland, Colorado, were fresh out of high school and were preaching an evangelistic meeting near Pikes Peak. Here is the story in his own words:

Before I was an ordained preacher, after I had finished the academy [high school] in Colorado, Brother Kenneth Gant and I were holding a meeting in a little town of about a hundred inhabitants up on the side of [Pikes] Peak. Our meeting place was an old dance pavilion that stuck out over one end of a little lake. We lived in a big empty house and had to do our own cooking. I had one room and Kenneth another, with just a cot and a trunk in each room. We cooked and ate in the kitchen—that is, we ate what we had there. And so we were living in this way. We were preaching there as best we knew how, and the people were interested.

There was a family with several little children, who lived in the finest home in town, and the father ran the biggest business in town. The mother came out to our meetings every night, bringing her children with her.

One Sunday afternoon Kenneth and I were visiting the people in their homes, inviting them to the meetings and praying and studying the Bible with them. When we called at this fine home, the husband was there, the wife was there, and a strange man was there also. After just a few words we excused ourselves and slipped away, because we didn't want to bother folks with company. You know the Bible says we are to testify "in season, out of season." That's right—"out of season." But we didn't testify out of season that day. We were just young fellows, and I suppose we hardly knew what to do, but we didn't say anything about Jesus at that house; we didn't say anything about salvation or heaven or about living for Christ and giving our hearts to Him. We just went away. That night the lady was not at the meeting, there in the front seat with her little children.

About five o'clock the next morning, Monday morning, I was awakened by Kenneth shaking my bed.

"Get up," he said, "get up. Something terrible has happened."

"What has happened?" I asked.

"Oh," he said, "Mrs. Brown committed suicide last night, and they are out there now dragging the lake to find her body."

And, sure enough, there was a man out there in a boat trying to pull her out of the water with a rake. She had become discouraged, left her home and husband and little children and everything, had climbed on a big post where our meeting place went out over the water, and had jumped in where it was deep. But that was not the worst of it. We ran over to our pavilion as fast as we could, and there she was, her body lying on our platform, covered with a sheet, right in the back of the pulpit—dead! And there on the pulpit desk was a note from that woman asking me to preach her funeral sermon. I had never preached a funeral sermon before in my life; that was to be my first. And the first thought that came into my mind was: "You were in the woman's home yesterday afternoon, but you didn't say anything about your Saviour; you didn't kneel down and pray in that home. You just made a little social call because there was company there. And now there she is—beyond prayer, beyond saving, beyond hope!" I want to tell you my friends, there were two young preachers who did a lot of thinking and praying and weeping before God that day. Whenever I think of it even yet, a deep shadow comes over my heart; still I believe that God in His mercy and providence allowed that experience to come to us.

Well, I have never worked on any sermon in all my life as I worked on that one. What could I say? I needed somebody to preach a sermon to me. But we tried, we prayed and worked together on that sermon. But, again in God's providence, when that woman's mother came up to the funeral from Colorado Springs, she brought a minister along to preach the funeral sermon....

You know, we always ought to be shining with the light from God's lighthouse. People ought to be seeing the reflection of that lighthouse in us.[3]

Prayer is generally appreciated by all. I have had neighbors tell me that they prefer not to talk about religion or the Bible. But whenever they are faced with a family emergency or life-and-death circumstances and I offer to pray, they are always grateful for prayer. Go in faith, making prayer your foundation, and God will abundantly bless your life. How do I know? He does it for me!

1. Ellen G. White, *The Great Controversy* (Nampa, ID: Pacific Press®, 2005), 525.

2. Ellen G. White, *Steps to Christ* (Washington, DC: Review and Herald®, 1977), 100.

3. H. M. S. Richards Sr., *Revival Sermons* (Washington, DC: Review and Herald®, 1947), 99–101.

8

THE POWER
OF TRUE FRIENDSHIP

I was talking to a friend about the fact that he knew so many people. He responded, "People either hate me or love me, there is no one in between. I say what I think and that rubs some people the wrong way. It is what it is."*

My friend's comments reminded me of the words of Solomon regarding friendship: "A man who has friends must himself be friendly, but there is a friend who sticks closer than a brother" (Proverbs 18:24).

If you are able in this life to have a friend with whom you can talk about anything, be at your worst and best, and still be loved and accepted as a friend, then you are a wealthy person.

In John 17, the Bible records a prayer of Jesus that He prayed just before He faced the Garden of Gethsemane and the cross. Verse 11 is a profound request of Jesus: "That they may be one as We are." Later, in verse 21, Jesus repeats the request: "That they all may be one, as You, Father, are in Me, and I in You; that they also may be one in Us, that the world may believe that You sent Me."

The oneness that Jesus prayed for was not a oneness of organization, administration, or obtaining unanimous votes at board meetings, although those things are OK too. Rather, it was a oneness of relationship. The union between Jesus and His Father was one of love

Portions of this chapter were adapted from Kurt Johnson, Prayer Works *(Nampa, ID: Pacific Press, 2001) and Kurt Johnson,* Successful Small Groups *(Hagerston, MD: Review & Herald, 2011).*

and working together. As Jesus went on to say in His prayer, "That the love with which You loved Me may be in them, and I in them" (John 17:26).

This love, this "getting along," can tear down barriers that people have erected between one another. This unity—this love—can convince the world that God and Christianity are for real. This is important! Why? Because it is more natural for people to be divided than united. It is more natural for people to fly apart than to come together. Real unity reveals itself as a "God thing" and not a "human thing."

As you visit people in various settings, pray that God will bind your heart with those whom you visit and with Himself, that a deep friendship will be developed that breaks down barriers and allows God to change lives. This can be done only through the Holy Spirit dwelling in your life and working upon the hearts and lives of those with whom you are visiting. This impact of the Holy Spirit comes only through prayer.

There are some basic friendship elements that help in establishing redemptive friendships. Redemptive friendship means that as fully devoted disciples of Jesus, we look for opportunities to share with our friends the truths of Scripture. These truths meet our needs in daily living and share the message of forgiveness and eternal life found in Jesus. The basic friendship elements are discussed in the following paragraphs.

Be friendly to others

I appreciate this statement: "People have to be drawn to you, whom they can see, before they can be drawn to Jesus, whom they cannot see."[1] Many times, we do not succeed in leading others to Christ because we do not take time to know the people with whom we are studying the Bible or visiting.

Live friendliness

When I was a teenager, my dad did not attend church on a regular basis. But our youth leader at church would drop us kids off at home after an event and come into our house and talk with Dad. The youth leader was a friendly man. He never pushed or coerced but talked about normal stuff and shared a hot or cold drink, depending on the weather. He would sometimes say to Dad, "The kids are conducting a program at church in two weeks. You should come and watch if you have time." And Dad would come.

Friendliness attracts like a magnet. A greeting, a smile, a polite gesture, a birthday card, and honest praise make a huge difference in letting people know you care.[2]

Remember that building relationships takes time

True friendships do not develop in a few days or weeks. Relationships build over time. I have a friend who loves gardening. I was visiting and noticed a tall floor rack sitting by the living room window that was loaded with healthy plants. My friend described the work and time it takes to care for the plants in order to keep them healthy. Friendship is the same.[3]

We read in *Gospel Workers*, "The Prince of teachers, He sought access to the people by the pathway of their most familiar associations. . . . He taught in a way that made them feel the completeness of His identification with their interests and happiness."[4]

Pay attention to people's needs

Everyone goes through a time of difficulty in their lives. All people have physical, social, and emotional needs and, at times, need a listening ear and kind support. If you can assist them in their trials of life, they will realize that God not only provides eternal life but also is able to meet every human need. You are the representative of Christ to them.[5]

Do not be in a hurry with people

We live in a world of *instant* everything. We send an email or text and are frustrated if we do not receive a reply in a few minutes. We apologize if it takes a couple of hours for us to respond. Remember postal mail—before email? It took several days to receive a response. We cannot wait five minutes for the burner on the stove to heat up our food, so we zap it in the microwave in two minutes.

It is easy to treat people the same way. In building relationships, we need to slow down and realize it takes time for friendships to develop and for people to grow spiritually. Jesus said that people are to be "born again" (John 3:3). A rebirth must happen for a person to become a Christian. The first birth—biological birth—took nine months. As parents, we wait for God's miracle-of-birth process to develop according to God's plan. We must do the same when it comes to spiritual birth and growth.[6]

Love people

The Bible simply states, "God is love" (1 John 4:8). People need to see God's love lived out in your life and mine. Some are skeptical and talk about the "hypocrites" in the church, so they stay away. In some cases, this reason is an excuse; but in other situations, it is true. Through the grace and power of Jesus Christ, let's be as loving, kind, and tenderhearted as possible.[7]

nvite friends to go places

Spend time with your Bible study families and others you are visiting outside of the regular visit times. Go shopping, on outings, share meals together, and include them in special events. Let them feel the warmth of your heart and see the love of Jesus reflected in your hospitality and kindness.[8]

Your local church members must be friendly

Your church family must be friendly, accepting, and appealing to the guests you invite to your church. Your personal effort will not be as successful if the congregation does not reflect the kindness and caring that you share with your Bible study interests. This ministry begins at the front door of the church with the greeters and continues through the foyer, into the sanctuary, and throughout the personal interaction that follows after the church service. If your church family could use a friendlier atmosphere, start by praying, and then begin to reach out with friendliness to other members. In time, and with the help of the Holy Spirit, the church will become a friendly place.[9]

Earn the trust of those you visit

Trust takes time. To build trust means you must share life with those you are visiting or studying the Bible with. This means that you need to talk as friends. You need to listen to what they say. Do not be impatient. If you want them to listen to you, then you need to listen to them too.[10]

Conclusion

If you and your local church family apply the preceding principles in your personal lives and show understanding, sympathy, and empathy with those whom God brings into your lives, then you will see individual making decisions to follow Jesus.

I appreciate this statement in *The Ministry of Healing*: "There is need of coming close to the people by personal effort. If less time were given to sermonizing, and more time were spent in personal ministry, greater results would be seen. The poor are to be relieved, the sick cared for the sorrowing and the bereaved comforted, the ignorant instructed the inexperienced counseled. We are to weep with those that weep and rejoice with those that rejoice. Accompanied by the power of persuasion, the power of prayer, the power of the love of God, this work will not, cannot, be without fruit."[11]

Pray daily for God to change your life to make you more like Jesus and to use you to introduce others to Him. I know He will do this for you because this is the will of God for your life and mine. So together let's agree that you will pray for me and I will pray for you as we share Jesus with a world in need of an eternal relationship with God.

1. *Disciple's Bible* (Madrid, Spain: Editorial Safliz SL, 2017), 1353. For more information see the section titled "Disciple's Resources" in *Disciple's Bible*. I have paraphrased some of the concepts in this chapter.

2. Disciple's Bible, 1353.

3. Disciple's Bible, 1353.

4. Ellen G. White, *Gospel Workers* (Hagerstown, MD: Review and Herald®, 2005), 45.

5. Disciple's Bible, 1353.

6. Disciple's Bible, 1353.

7. Disciple's Bible, 1353.

8. Disciple's Bible, 1354.

9. Disciple's Bible, 1354.

10. Disciple's Bible, 1353, 1354.

11. Ellen G. White, *The Ministry of Healing* (Mountain View, CA: Pacific Press®, 1942), 143, 144.